AF570798

DISCOVERING OUR WORLD

Science Activities and Worksheets for Young Children

by Rosie Seaman

Fearon Teacher Aids
a division of
David S. Lake Publishers
Belmont, California

About the Author

Rosie Soto Seaman is well known along the Gulf Coast as an author, educator, and television producer. She is the Director of Children's Programming for WKRG-TV in Mobile, Alabama. She has been involved with *Rosie's Place, Small Fry News,* and *Youth Magazine,* three long-running, award-winning children's programs. Rosie has also received regional acclaim for her art, early childhood, and special education courses.

Illustrated by Duane Bibby

Entire contents copyright © 1987 by David S. Lake Publishers, 500 Harbor Boulevard, Belmont, California 94002. Permission is hereby granted to reproduce the materials in this book for noncommercial classroom use.

ISBN 0-8224-1926-2

Printed in the United States of America

1. 9 8 7 6 5 4

Contents

Teacher's Guide

Look Around You, page 7

Concept: There are many things in our world. (We can see, smell, touch, and listen to them.)

Lesson: Take the children on a discovery walk. Along the way emphasize different approaches. For example, have the children listen for the sounds of nature. Ask them to close their eyes and listen. You might ask them to identify the sounds or where they came from. Children should also try touching and smelling the things around them. They should record on the worksheet something they saw, heard, felt, or smelled.

Living or Nonliving? page 8

Concept: Living things are different from nonliving things.

Lesson: Make two posters or murals with the children. Let them use magazines to find pictures of living things and nonliving things. Ask the children to cut these pictures out, and help the children paste them onto the posters. Label the posters "These Are Living Things" and "These Are Nonliving Things." Use the worksheet to reinforce the concept.

There Are Many Kinds of Living Things, page 9

Concept: There are many different kinds of living things.

Lesson: Take the children on a discovery walk. Ask them to point out all the different living things they see. Reinforce the idea that there are many kinds of living things. Use the worksheet to underscore this idea.

There Are Many Kinds of Nonliving Things, page 10

Concept: There are many different kinds of nonliving things.

Lesson: Ask the children to point out nonliving things in the classroom. Then take the children on a neighborhood walk. Ask them to point out all the different nonliving things they see. Use the worksheet to reinforce the idea that there are many different kinds of nonliving things.

A Season Book, page 11

Concept: There are four seasons. (We call them spring, summer, winter, and fall.)

Lesson: Collect pictures that show characteristics of the four seasons. (Calendars and postcards are good sources for pictures.) Show the pictures and discuss each season. Ask children what they like best about each season. Use the worksheet to reinforce the idea that there are four seasons.

Winter Wonders, page 12

Concept: There are certain things we associate with winter.

Lesson: Use a calendar to show when winter occurs. Ask children to name some of the characteristics of winter. Discuss their answers and point out some of the holidays and events that occur during this season. Use the worksheet to reinforce the concept.

Spring Signs, page 13

Concept: There are certain things we associate with spring.

Lesson: Use a calendar to show when spring occurs. Ask children to name some of the characteristics of spring. Discuss their answers and point out some of the holidays and events that occur during this season. Use the worksheet to reinforce the concept.

Summer Specials, page 14

Concept: There are certain things we associate with summer.

Lesson: Use a calendar to show when summer occurs. Ask children to name some of the characteristics of summer. Discuss their answers and point out some of the holidays and events that occur during this season. Use the worksheet to reinforce the concept.

Fall Features, page 15

Concept: There are certain things we associate with fall.

Lesson: Use a calendar to show when fall occurs. Ask children to name some of the characteristics of fall. Discuss their answers and point out some of the holidays and events that occur during this season. Use the worksheet to reinforce the concept.

Air Is All Around Us, page 16

Concept: Air is all around us even though we cannot see it.

Lesson: Show children a clear plastic bottle and ask them whether they see anything in the bottle. Then hold the bottle near a child's face and squeeze it. Ask children whether the bottle was really empty or whether the child felt something escaping from it. Reinforce the idea using other bottles, balloons, and plastic bags. Use the worksheet to underscore the idea.

We Need Air, page 17

Concept: We need air to live.

Lesson: Ask children if they have any air in their bodies. Tell them to test this by holding a hand near their noses and mouths while they breathe. Ask them if they feel anything escaping from their bodies. Discuss the fact that we need air to live. Have children cover their noses and mouths and hold their breaths. When they have to take a breath, ask them why they let air into their bodies. Use the worksheet to reinforce the idea that many living things need air to live.

We Need Clean Air, page 18

Concept: It is important not to pollute the air.

Lesson: Use pictures to illustrate what air pollution is and what causes it. Discuss with children why air pollution is undesirable and harmful. Lead children into a discussion about the ways in which they can help stop air pollution. For example, whenever possible they should ride a bike or walk rather than riding in a car. Use the worksheet to reinforce the concept.

Air Fills Things, page 19

Concept: Air can be used to inflate objects.

Lesson: Blow up a balloon. Ask children what made the balloon get bigger. Let the air back out. Ask children to describe what happened. Have them think of different things that air can fill. Use the worksheet to reinforce the concept that air can inflate objects.

Wind Is Moving Air, page 20

Concept: Wind is moving air.

Lesson: Hand out paper fans or cardboard pieces to the children. Ask them whether they can feel any wind in the room. Help children discover that they can make a wind using the fans or cardboard. Discuss ways in which people can use wind. Use the worksheet to reinforce the ideas.

We Can See Wind, page 21

Concept: We can see the effects of wind moving.

Lesson: Let the children look outside. Ask them if the wind is blowing. Explain that we can see the wind blow when we look at objects like flags. When there is no wind, the flag does not move. When there is wind, the flag moves. Ask children what other things we could look at to see if the wind is blowing. Use the worksheet to reinforce the concept.

Water Is Important! page 22

Concept: We use water for many things.

Lesson: Ask children what they have used water for today. Also ask them if they can think of other things they use water for. Discuss their answers and explain why water is important. Let children cut pictures out of magazines that show water being used. Use the worksheet to reinforce the idea that we use water for many things.

Float or Sink? page 23

Concept: Some things float on water and some things sink.

Lesson: Obtain a basin of water, some objects that float (leaves, twigs, ping-pong balls), and some objects that sink (keys, rocks, marbles). Explain to the children that each object will either float or sink in the water. Have them guess what each object will do. Test each object. Use the worksheet to reinforce the concept.

Keep the Water Clean! page 24

Concept: It is important not to pollute our water.

Lesson: Use pictures to illustrate what water pollution is and what causes it. Discuss with children why water pollution is undesirable and harmful. Lead children into a discussion about ways in which they can help stop water pollution. For example, they should never throw trash into a river, lake, or ocean. Use the worksheet to reinforce the idea that water pollution is harmful.

What Do We Use When It Rains? page 25

Concept: We wear different items depending on the weather.

Lesson: Bring in several articles of clothing that would be appropriate for different weather conditions (raincoat, mittens, swimsuit). Hold up each article of clothing and ask children when we would wear the items. Also ask children to tell you what other things they would use when it rains. Use the worksheet to reinforce the concept.

The Colors of a Rainbow, page 26

Concept: The colors of a rainbow always appear in the same order—red, orange, yellow, green, blue, and violet.

Lesson: Create a rainbow by placing a prism in a window that has a light beam shining through it. Place a piece of white paper under the projected rainbow so children can study it. Ask the children to name the colors they see. Have them arrange strips of colored paper in the same order as the colors of the rainbow. Move the prism. Ask the children if the order of the colors changed. Use the worksheet to reinforce what the colors are and their order.

Snow Is Made of Water, page 27

Concept: Snow is made of water.

Lesson: Let the children fill a pan with snow. (If there is no snow in your area you can do this with shaved ice.) Bring the pan indoors and have the children watch the snow melt. Ask the children what snow is made of and why it melted. Discuss their answers. You might also have them look at individual snowflakes. Use the worksheet to reinforce the concept that snowflakes come in different shapes.

Hot and Cold, page 28

Concept: Some things are hot, and some things are cold. We use a thermometer to measure how hot or cold something is.

Lesson: Bring a thermometer to class and discuss it. Point out the numbers on the outside and the liquid on the inside. Tell children that hot things will make the liquid rise and cold things will make the liquid drop. Demonstrate using glasses of hot and cold water. Use the worksheet to reinforce the idea that some things are hot and some are cold.

Some Things Give Us Light, page 29

Concept: There are many sources of light.

Lesson: Write the word *light* on the board. Ask the children to name all the things they can think of that give us light. You might ask questions such as, What gives us light during the day? What gives us light in this room? What gives us light at night? Discuss what happens when there is no light. Use the worksheet to reinforce the concept.

We Make Some Lights, page 30

Concept: Some lights are made by people, and some are not.

Lesson: Bring in pictures of different light sources (sun, lamps, moon, fireflies, fire, flashlights). Ask children which ones they think are made by people. Discuss the differences between natural light sources and light sources that are made by people. Use the worksheet to reinforce the concept.

Find the Shadow, page 31

Concept: Shadows are made when objects get in the way of light.

Lesson: Cut some shapes out of paper. Put each shape in front of a light source. Explain that the "darkness" is called a shadow. Turn off the light. Ask children if they think you can still make a shadow. Let them try. Turn on the light and let them try again. Point out that a shadow is roughly the same shape as the object that stops the light. Use the worksheet to reinforce this idea.

What Do We Hear? page 32

Concept: We hear many different sounds.

Lesson: Tape-record familiar noises, such as fire engines, a dog barking, an alarm clock, a ball bouncing, a plane flying, a bird singing, a baby crying, and a door slamming. Have the children try to identify each sound. Ask them to think of other sounds they have heard. Use the worksheet to reinforce the concept that there are many different sounds.

Vibrations Cause Sounds, page 33

Concept: Sound is caused by vibrations.

Lesson: Place a ruler on the edge of a table with most of the ruler extended over the edge. Hold it firmly with one hand and let a child hit the free end. Ask children to describe what they saw and heard. Explain that the up and down motion is called vibration. Explain that all sound is caused by vibration. Let the children experiment with the ruler to create different sounds. Use the worksheet to reinforce the concept.

Sound Can Travel, page 34

Concept: Sound waves travel through objects.

Lesson: Obtain a large pan of water. Let a child drop a penny in the center of the pan. Ask the children to describe what they see. Also have them describe the way the waves moved. Compare these waves to sound waves. (The waves moved in a circular pattern away from the penny; sound waves move in a circular pattern away from the object that makes the sound.) Use the worksheet to reinforce the idea that sounds travel.

Tools Can Help Us, page 35

Concept: Tools make certain things easier for us to do.

Lesson: Bring several small tools to class (hammer, toothbrush, fork, screwdriver). Ask children what each tool helps us to do. Discuss their answers. Stress that tools help people do things that would be much harder to do without them. Use the worksheet to reinforce the concept.

Machines Can Help Us, page 36

Concept: Machines can save people time and effort.

Lesson: Collect pictures of different machines. Explain that people invented and built these machines to do things that are difficult to do. Ask the children to tell you what each machine does and how it helps people. Use the worksheet to reinforce the idea that there are many types of machines.

Machines Can Move Us, page 37

Concept: Certain machines can help us move from one place to another.

Lesson: Ask children to tell how they got to school today. Then ask them if they have ever been on a bicycle, a train, a plane, or a boat. Explain that all of these are machines that help us move from one place to another. Let the children cut out pictures from magazines that show forms of transportation. Use the worksheet to reinforce the concept.

There Are Many Kinds of Rocks, page 38

Concept: There are many different kinds of rocks.

Lesson: Bring different types of rocks to class. (You might also bring pictures of hard-to-find rocks.) Discuss the rocks, pointing out the similarities and differences. Ask children which rocks they like the best. Use the worksheet to reinforce the concept.

Large or Small? page 39

Concept: The size of rocks varies greatly.

Lesson: Bring in samples and pictures of rocks that will give children a realistic concept of their relative sizes. Let the children discuss different rocks that they have seen. Point out that we often call small rocks *pebbles* and large rocks *boulders.* Use the worksheet to reinforce the concept.

Rocks Are Useful, page 40

Concept: Rocks are used to make many things—roads, buildings, bridges.

Lesson: Make a poster or mural with the children. Let them use magazines to find pictures of things made of rock. Ask the children to cut these pictures out, and help them paste the pictures onto the poster. Label the poster "Rocks Are Useful." Use the worksheet to reinforce the uses of rocks.

This Is the Earth, page 41

Concept: The earth is a planet with land areas and water areas.

Lesson: Display a globe. Explain that the earth is like the globe except it is much bigger. Point out the land and water areas on the globe. Help children find the area in which they live. Use the worksheet to reinforce the concept.

Night and Day, page 42

Concept: The position of the earth and sun and the rotation of the earth cause night and day.

Lesson: Bring in a high-intensity lamp and a globe. Ask the children to think of the lamp as the sun and the globe as the earth. Darken the room and hold the globe in the path of the light. Have the children observe the globe from the side. Discuss which side indicates night and which indicates day. Mark a spot on the globe with a piece of tape. Illustrate the rotation of the earth by slowly turning the globe. Help children formulate the idea that we move from the dark area into the light area and back again each day.

The Earth Moves Around the Sun, page 43

Concept: The earth revolves around the sun.

Lesson: Bring in a high-intensity lamp and a globe. Ask the children to think of the lamp as the sun and the globe as the earth. Illustrate the revolution of the earth around the sun. Use the worksheet to reinforce the concept.

The Phases of the Moon, page 44

Concept: The moon goes through different phases.

Lesson: Cut cardboard shapes that represent the phases of the moon. Hold up each shape and ask the children if they have ever seen the moon when it looks like the shape. Tell them the name for each shape. Use the worksheet to reinforce the concept.

Name ______________________________

Look Around You

Draw a picture of something you discovered on your walk. Color the picture. Trace the words.

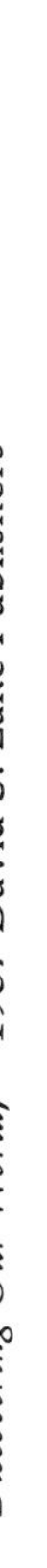
Discovering Our World, © 1987 David S. Lake Publishers

Our world is full of things.

Name ______________________

Living or Nonliving?

There are many things in our world. Some are living. Some are nonliving. Cut and then paste the pictures in the correct places. Trace the words. Color the pictures.

Discovering Our World, © 1987 David S. Lake Publishers

Name ______________________________

There Are Many Kinds of Living Things

Color the pictures. In each row, circle the living thing that is different.

Discovering Our World, © 1987 David S. Lake Publishers

Name ______________________________

There Are Many Kinds of Nonliving Things

Find the nonliving things. Color them.

Discovering Our World, © 1987 David S. Lake Publishers

Name ______________________________

A Season Book

Make your own book. Trace the words. Cut out the pictures. Staple the pages together.

Discovering Our World, © 1987 David S. Lake Publishers

Name ______________________________

Winter Wonders

Connect the dots from 1 to 10 to find something you might see in the winter. Color the picture.

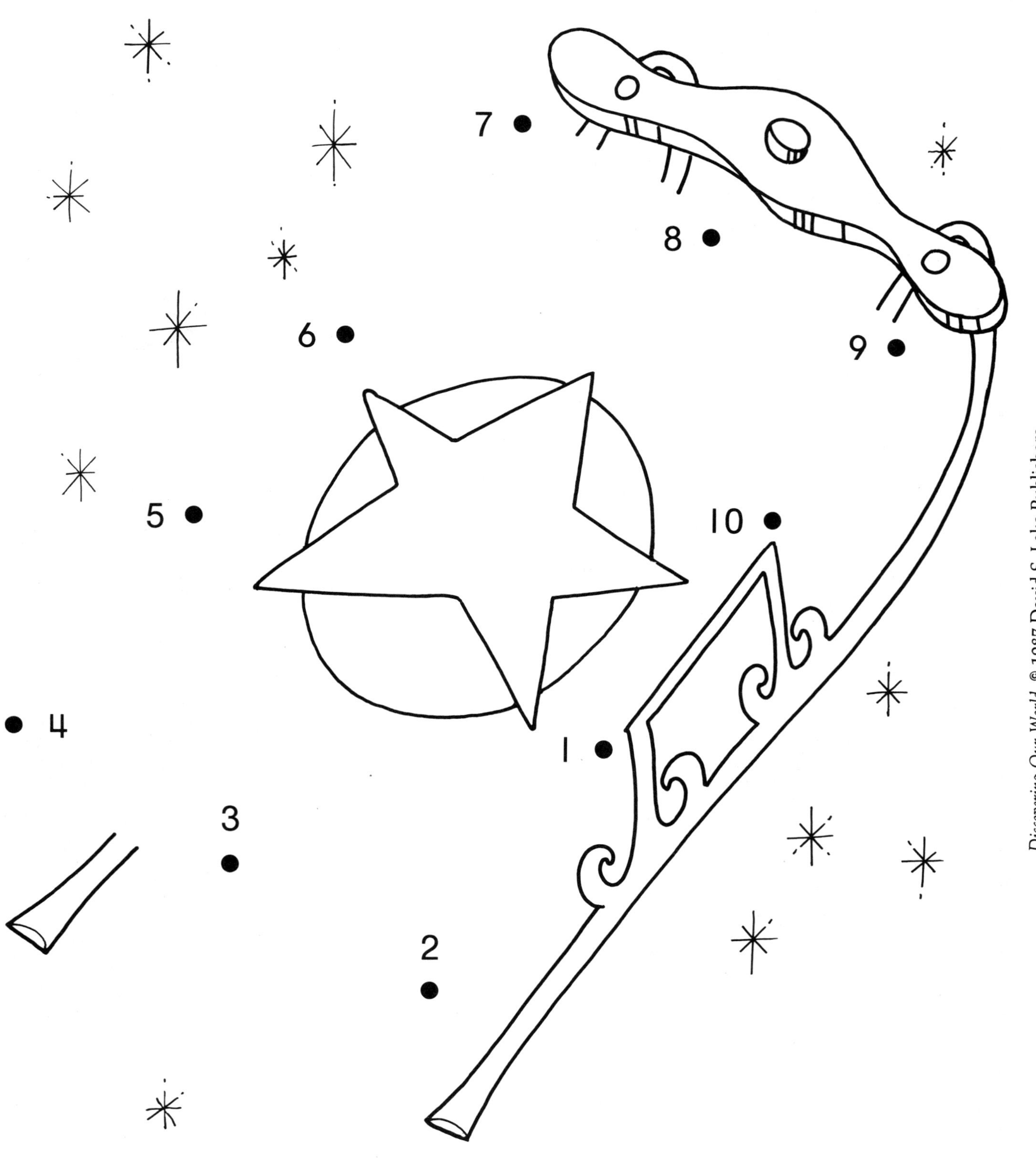

Discovering Our World, © 1987 David S. Lake Publishers

Name ______________________________

Spring Signs

In each row, find two things that are exactly alike. Color them the same way. Color the other spring things.

Discovering Our World, © 1987 David S. Lake Publishers

Name ____________________________

Summer Specials

Summer is the time to play. Draw a line between the summer things that match. Color the pictures.

Discovering Our World, © 1987 David S. Lake Publishers

Name ______________________________

Fall Features

Find the things that happen in the fall. Color them.

Discovering Our World, © 1987 David S. Lake Publishers

Name ______________________________

Air Is All Around Us

Color the pictures. Trace the words.

Air is all around us.

Discovering Our World, © 1987 David S. Lake Publishers

Name ______________________________

We Need Air

Find all the things that need air. Circle them. Color the pictures. Trace the words.

Living things need air.

Discovering Our World, © 1987 David S. Lake Publishers

Name ______________________________

We Need Clean Air

Find all the things that make the air dirty. Put an X on them. Color the pictures. Trace the words.

We need clean air!

Discovering Our World, © 1987 David S. Lake Publishers

Name ______________________________

Air Fills Things

In each row, find the object that is filled with air. Color it red. Use other colors for the rest of the objects.

Discovering Our World, © 1987 David S. Lake Publishers

Name ________________________________

Wind Is Moving Air

Find something fun to do on windy days. Color the spaces.

1 = Green 2 = Red 3 = Yellow

Discovering Our World, © 1987 David S. Lake Publishers

Name ______________________________

We Can See Wind

Trace the words. Cut and then paste the labels to match the pictures. Color the pictures.

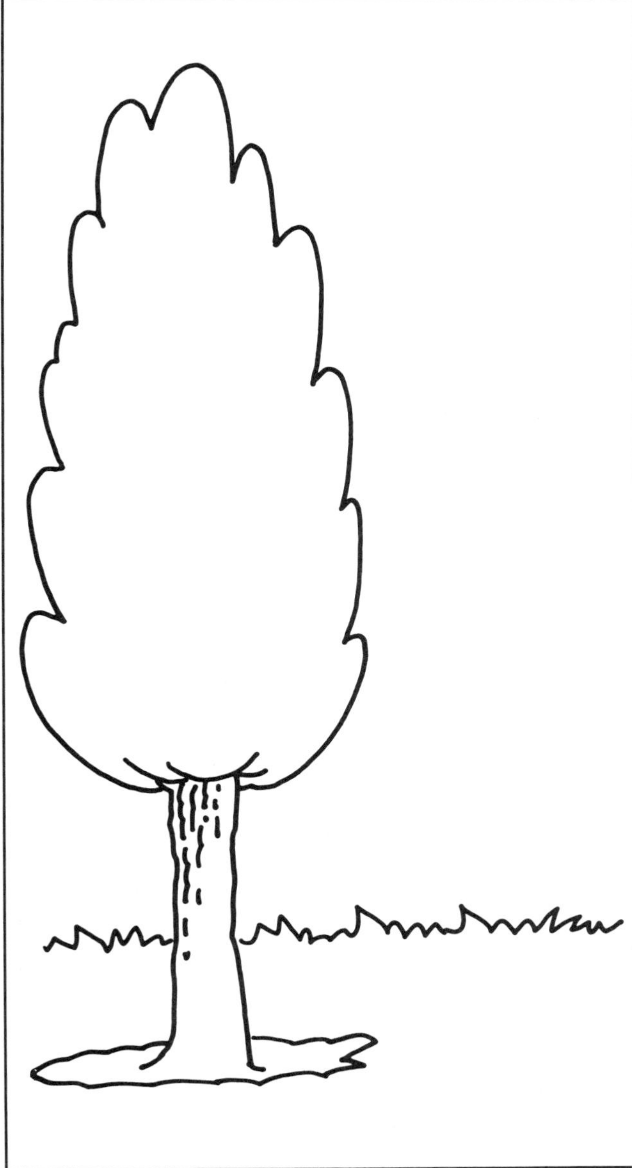

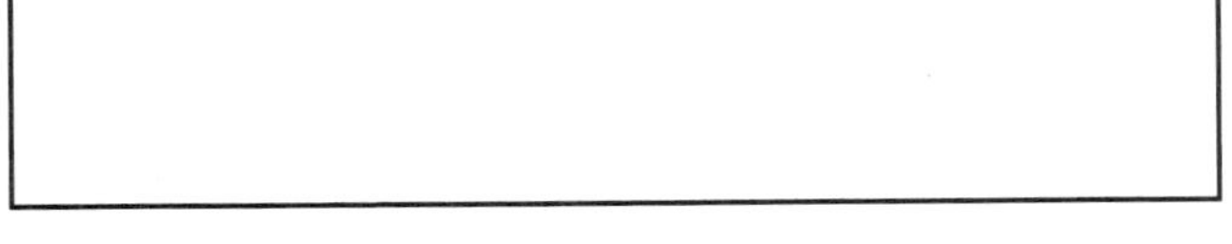

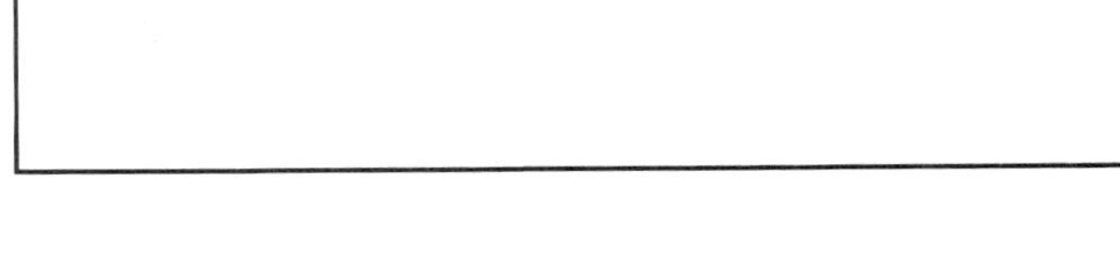

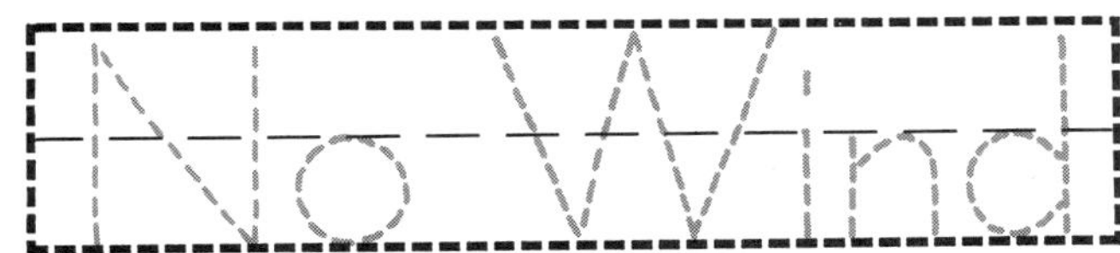

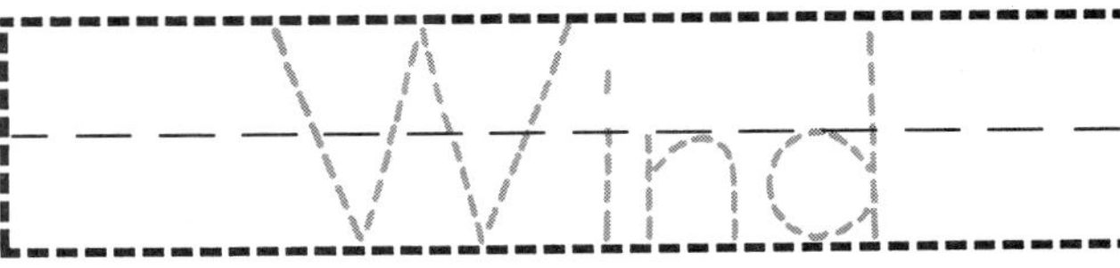

Discovering Our World, © 1987 David S. Lake Publishers

Name ______________________________

Water Is Important!

We use water every day. Find all the pictures that show water being used. Color them.

Discovering Our World, © 1987 David S. Lake Publishers

Name ______________________________

Float or Sink?

Cut and paste here the objects that are floating on the water.

Cut and paste here the objects that have sunk in the water.

Discovering Our World, © 1987 David S. Lake Publishers

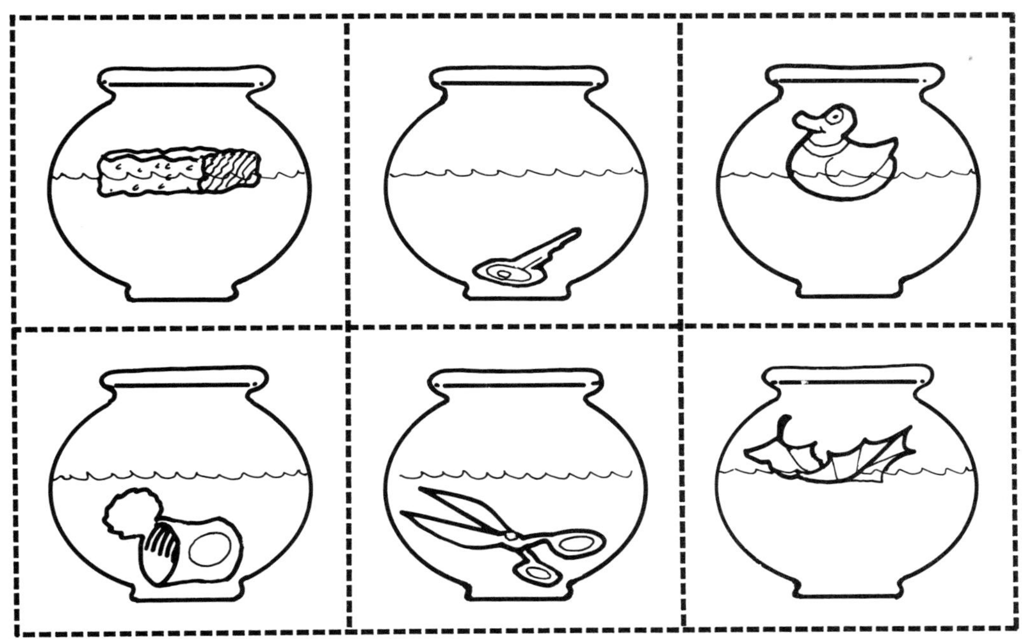

Name ______________________________

Keep the Water Clean!

Help Freddy the Fish get past the bad things that don't belong in the water. Connect the dots from 1 to 10 to get Freddy home safely. Color the picture.

Discovering Our World, © 1987 David S. Lake Publishers

Name ______________________________

What Do We Use When It Rains?

Circle the things we use when it rains. Color them.

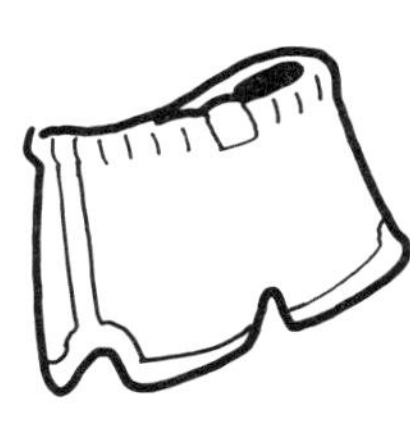
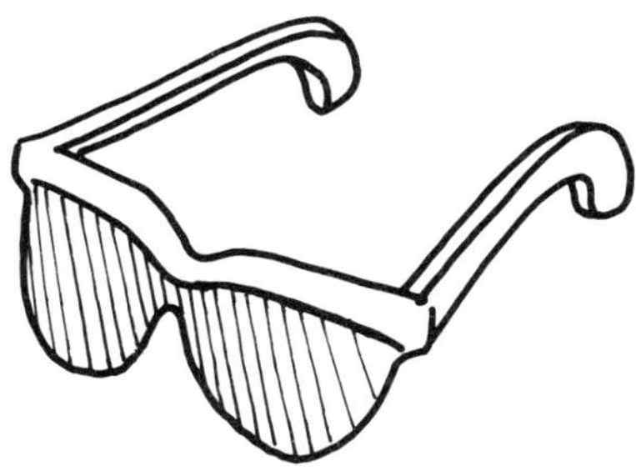

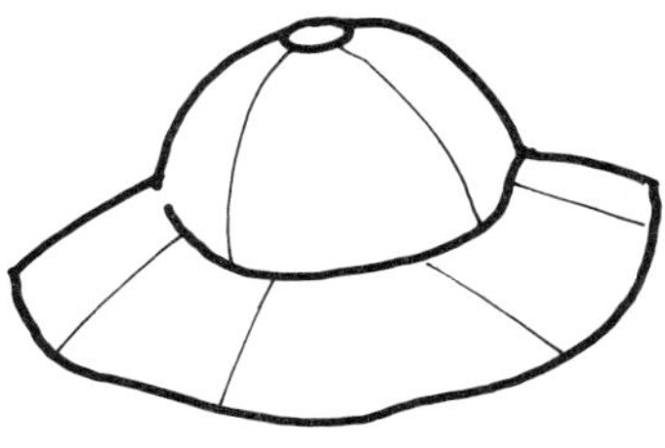

Discovering Our World, © 1987 David S. Lake Publishers

Name ______________________________

The Colors of a Rainbow

A rainbow has appeared! Trace each word. Then color the rainbow.

red orange yellow

green blue violet

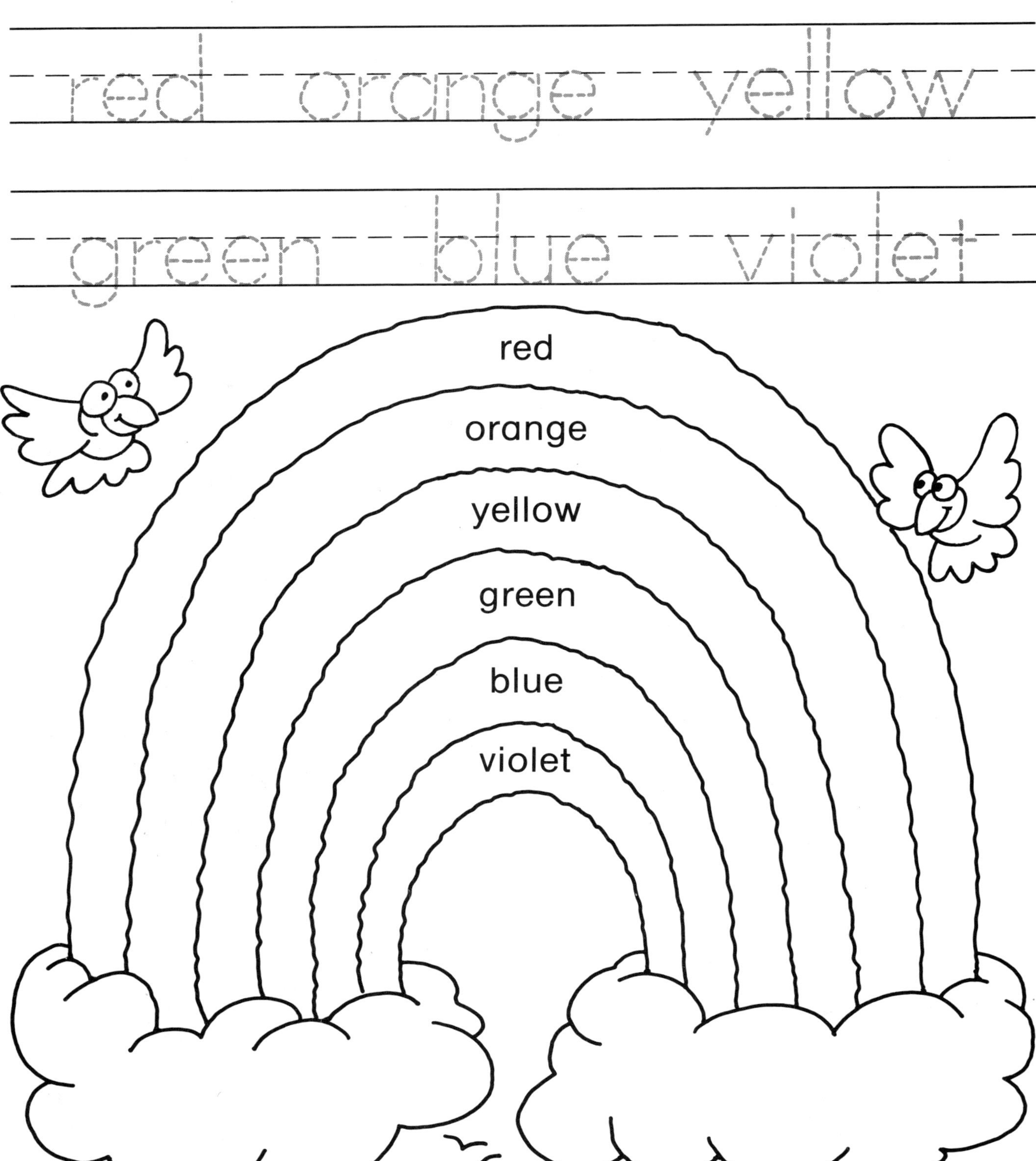

Discovering Our World, © 1987 David S. Lake Publishers

Name ______________________________

Snow Is Made of Water

Look at each row. One snowflake is different. Circle it. Color the snowflakes.

  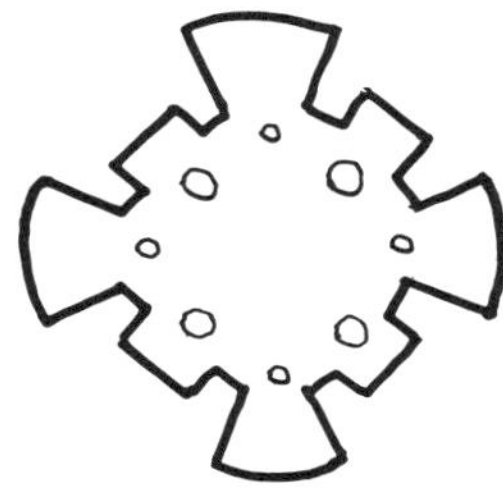 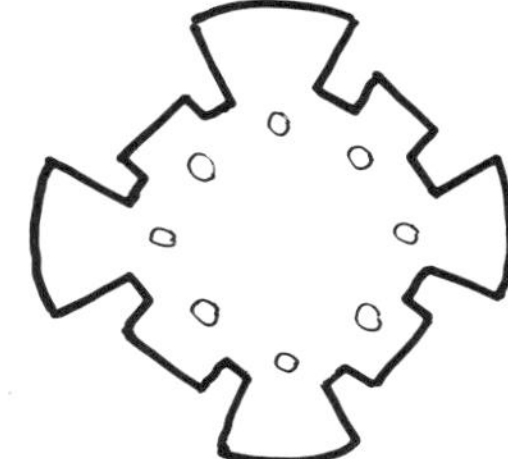

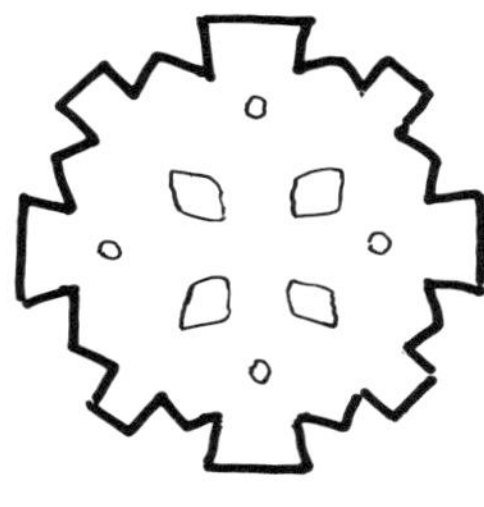 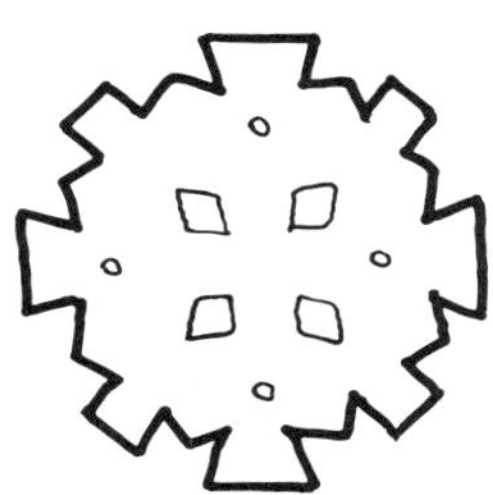  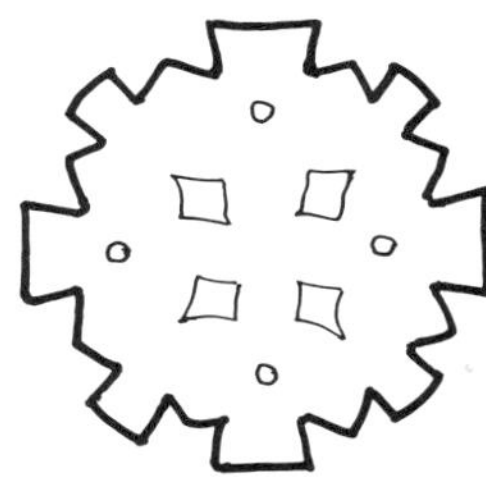

Discovering Our World, © 1987 David S. Lake Publishers

Name ____________________

Hot and Cold

Some things are hot. Some things are cold. Cut and then paste the pictures in the correct places. Trace the words. Color the pictures.

hot   cold

Discovering Our World, © 1987 David S. Lake Publishers

Name ______________________________

Some Things Give Us Light

Look at the pictures. Find the things that give us light. Circle them. Color the pictures.

Discovering Our World, © 1987 David S. Lake Publishers

Name ______________________

We Make Some Lights

Find all the pictures of lights made by people. Circle them. Color the pictures. Trace the words.

Many things give light.

Discovering Our World, © 1987 David S. Lake Publishers

Name ______________________________

Find the Shadow

Jacob is missing his shadow. Trace the dotted lines to find his shadow. Find another shadow. Color the shadows black. Color the rest of the picture.

Discovering Our World, © 1987 David S. Lake Publishers

Name ______________________________

What Do We Hear?

Find the pictures of sounds you have heard. Color them. Trace the words.

I hear these sounds.

Discovering Our World, © 1987 David S. Lake Publishers

Name ____________________

Vibrations Cause Sounds

Color the pictures. Trace the words.

No Sound

Sound

Discovering Our World, © 1987 David S. Lake Publishers

Name ______________________________

Sound Can Travel

Color the pictures. Cut and then paste the pictures to show how sound travels.

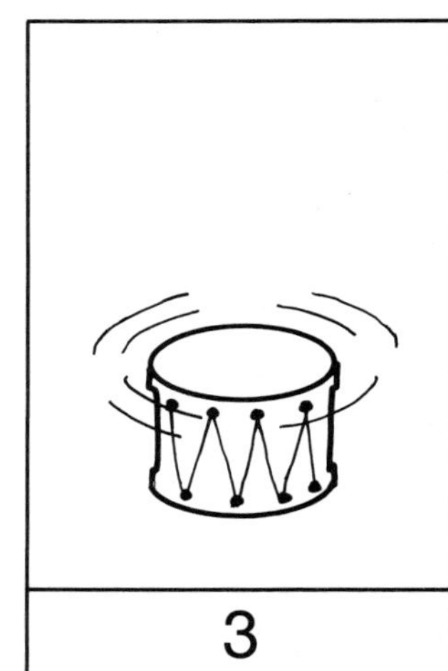

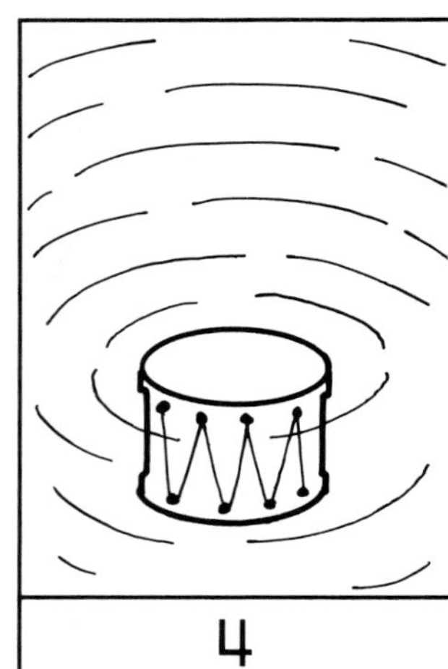

Discovering Our World, © 1987 David S. Lake Publishers

Name ______________________________

Tools Can Help Us

Color the pictures. Cut and then paste the pictures to show the tool you would use with each object.

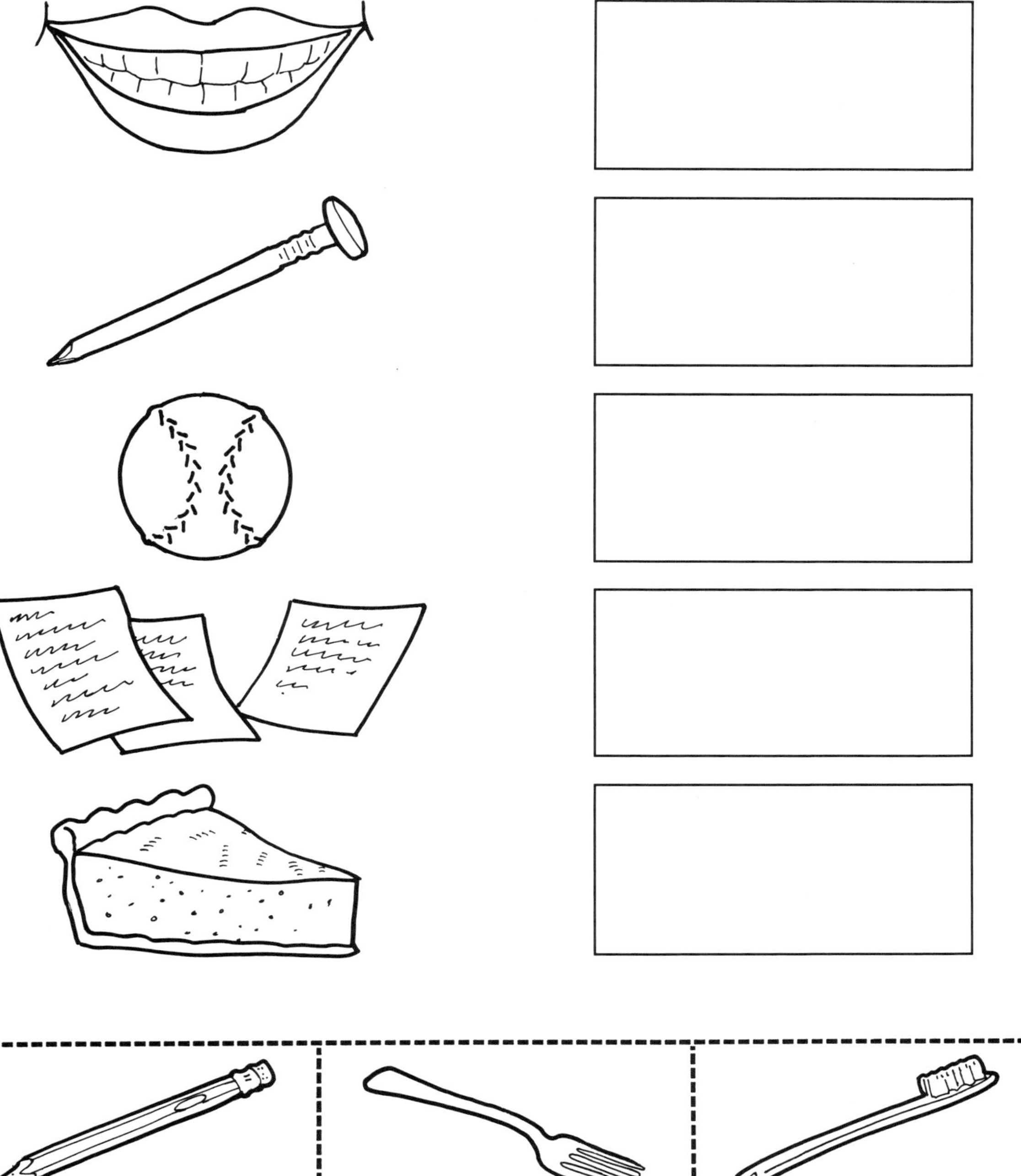

Discovering Our World, © 1987 David S. Lake Publishers

Name ______________________________

Machines Can Help Us

Find all the machines. Circle them. Color the pictures. Trace the words.

Machines can help us.

Discovering Our World, © 1987 David S. Lake Publishers

Name ______________________________

Machines Can Move Us

In each row, find the machines that help us move. Color them.

   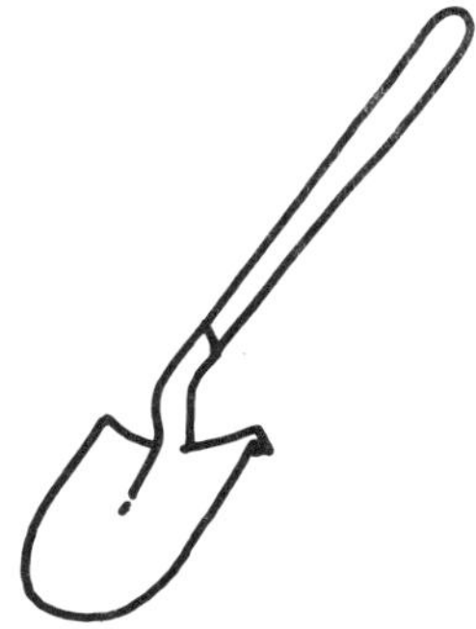

Discovering Our World, © 1987 David S. Lake Publishers

Name ______________________________

There Are Many Kinds of Rocks

Draw a line between the rocks that match. Color the pictures.

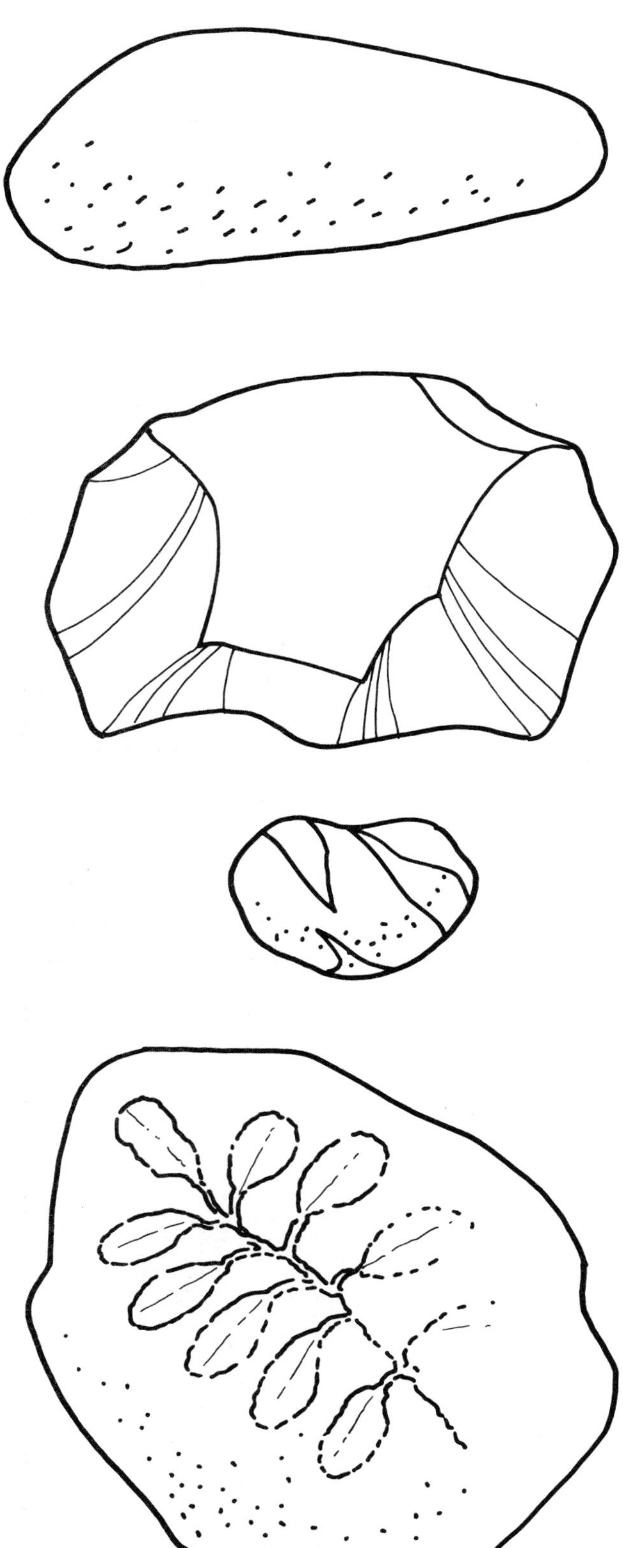

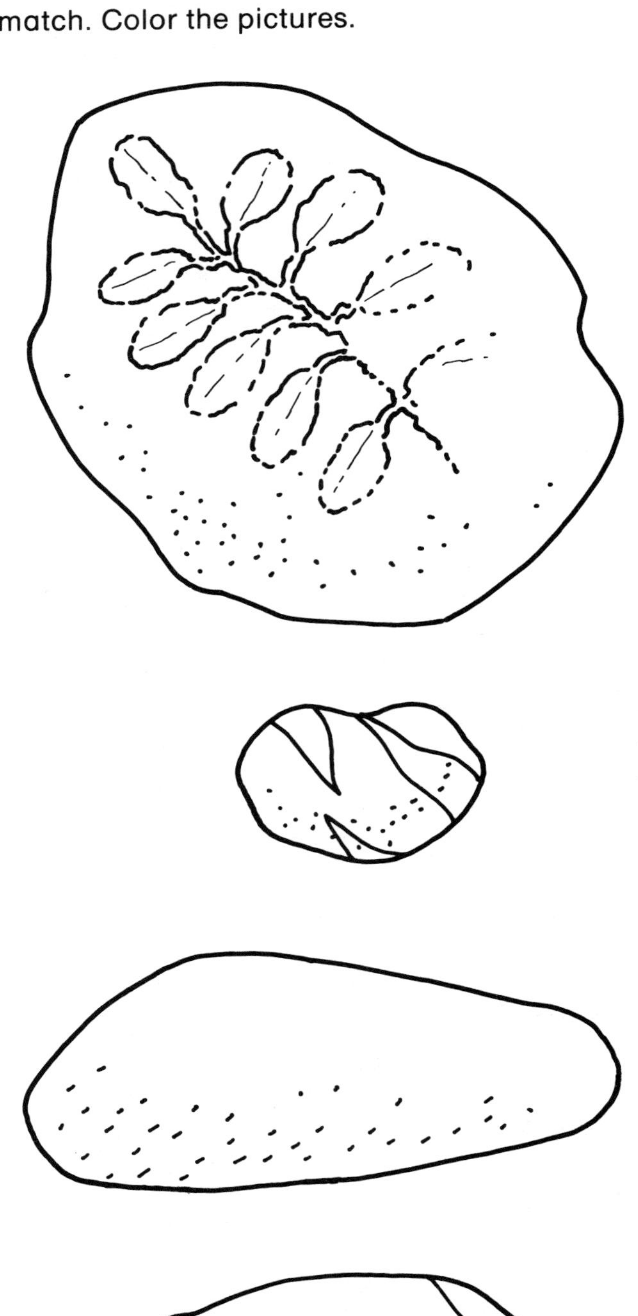

Discovering Our World, © 1987 David S. Lake Publishers

Name ____________________

Large or Small?

Color the rocks. Cut and then paste the pictures to show the sizes of the rocks. Trace the words.

small medium large

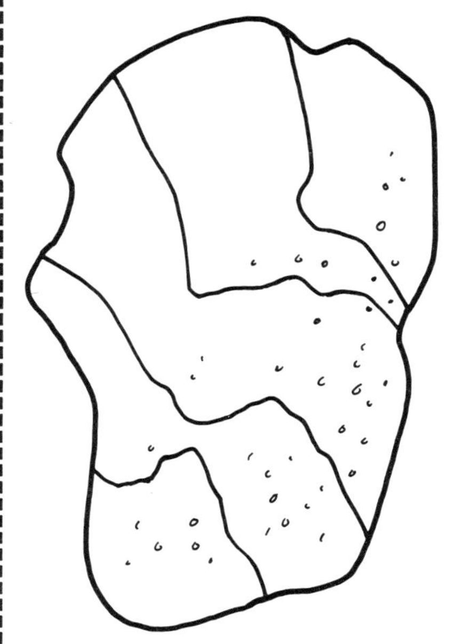

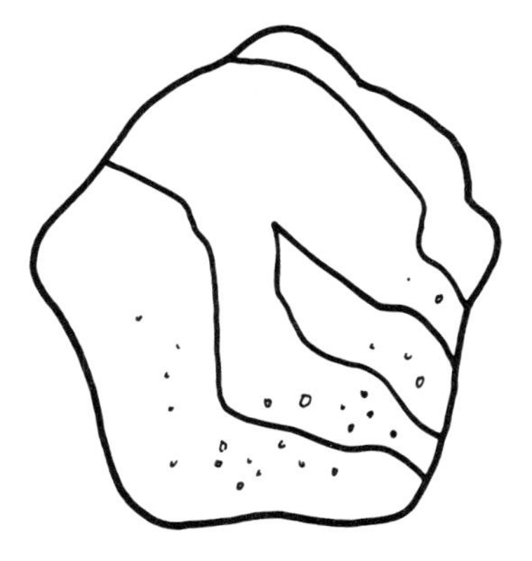

Discovering Our World, © 1987 David S. Lake Publishers

Name ______________________________

Rocks Are Useful

Look at the picture. Find the things we use rocks for. Color them.

Discovering Our World, © 1987 David S. Lake Publishers

Name ______________________________

This Is the Earth

Color the land brown. Color the water blue. Trace the words.

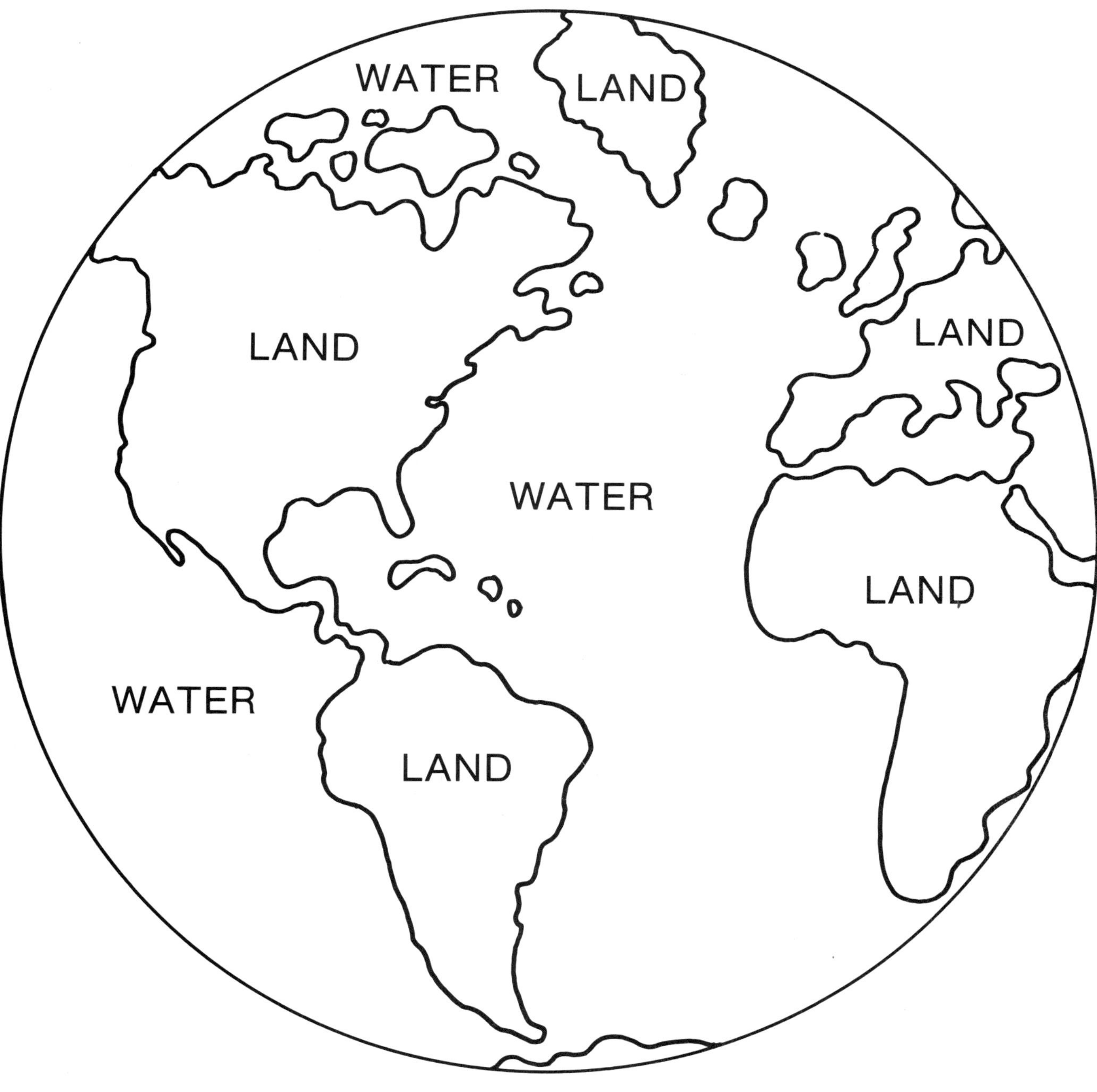

Discovering Our World, © 1987 David S. Lake Publishers

The earth is our home.

Name ______________________________

Night and Day

Trace the words. Cut and then paste the labels. Color the pictures.

Day | Night

Discovering Our World, © 1987 David S. Lake Publishers

Name ______________________________

The Earth Moves Around the Sun

Trace the dotted lines to complete the picture. Color the picture.
Trace the words.

The path of the earth

Discovering Our World, © 1987 David S. Lake Publishers

Name ________________________________

The Phases of the Moon

Color the pictures. Cut and then paste the pictures in the correct places.

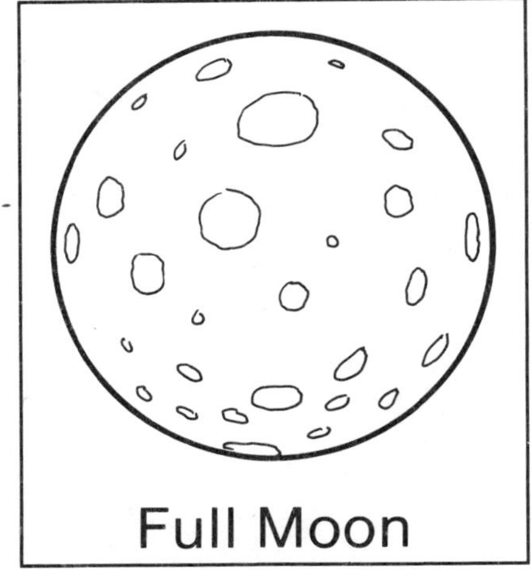

Full Moon

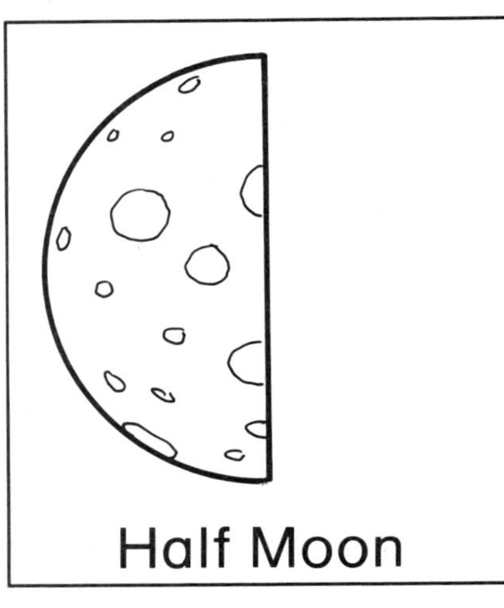

Half Moon

Crescent Moon

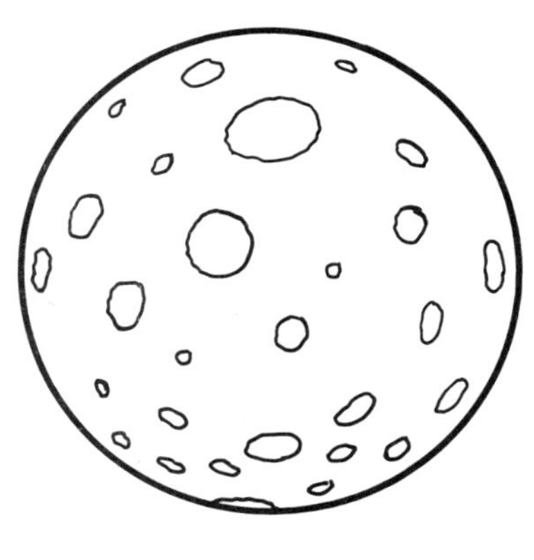

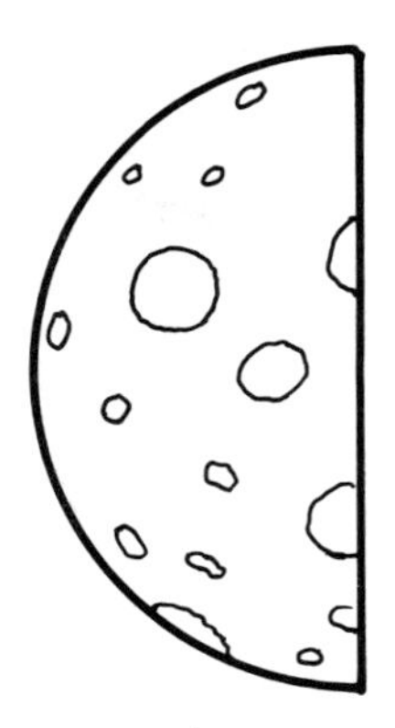

Discovering Our World, © 1987 David S. Lake Publishers